UNBOUNDED

An Inner Sense of Destiny

J. J. BHATT

ISBN: 9798642213148

Title:

Unbounded

Author:

J.J. Bhatt

Published and Distributed by Amazon and Kindle worldwide.

This book is manufactured in the Unites States of America.

PREFACE

Unbounded: an Inner Sense of Destiny probes into human nature, human episodes and futuristic vision. It intends to evoke the detrimental consequences of the *thinking non-human machines* and to bring attention to the prevailing silent alienation as we have been imperceptibly losing control over our privacy, our dignity and in fact over our destiny.

Against this backdrop, *Unbounded: an Inner Sense of Destiny* encourages in rewriting the story of humanity according to what sort of world we all want. It is time we reinvigorate our self-confidence for we have the capacity to define ourselves as an embodiment of rational and moral will to direct our own destiny. In this respect, let each of us emerge as our own unbounded hero in life. Specifically, let each of us join others like-minded for the collective purpose of unity, courage, hope and integrity in order to bring forth positive changes in the world. In such a noble quest, it is paramount we learn to listen to one another and be friends rather than strangers. Let us also learn how to stand tall as an *Enlightened Global Spirit* for the sake of our children's future. Let us at least learn how to walk the walk before it is too late.

3

UNBOUNDED: an Inner Sense of Destiny is my eleventh book comprised of poetic expressions. Like the previously published titles, it expresses thoughts akin to the world famous inspiring falls: the vibrant Niagara, majestic Iguassu and the magnificent Victoria. I must confess that natural flow of waters has always fascinated me since childhood whence the preferred format in this book as well.

                                        J.J. Bhatt

CONTENTS

Unbounded

Unbounded
Is mighty
Human who's a
Relevant player in
The game of
Trials and errors

Though
Temporal he's
Determined
To break out of the
Cocoon to make it
All through

He's an
Intelligent being
Don't let him
Constrained by
False narratives
Of his time

He's an
Invincible spirit
Let him
Spark
Enlightenment...

9

Inspiration

A thin
Thread of snap
That's what life
Happens to be

An
Inner sense
Of destiny where
Dream must turn
To reality

Unbounded
Being
An overture
Of moral will

Unbounded
Being
What an
Expression of
Perfection
To be realized
Soon...

Stand
Tall

All
Fragmented
Point of views
Must be
Woven together
Before
Our indefatigable
Journey begins

Let's
Bring breathe
Of fresh vision into
Our chaotic existence
Before we take the
First step

Let
There evolve
A spirit of
Universal validity,
"We're
Infinite possibilities"

Let's
Be reborn in
Simplicity and
Moral will to be...

On the Edge

Being
Not in a place
Where he
Ought to be
Today

Being
Forlorned
From
Nature
While trapped
Into
The sphere of
Insecured
Feelings

Being
Caught in a
World where
Mercurial change
Is threatening
His inner being...

Vision 20/20

Man
Mustn't exists
In a mistaken
Illusion of
His reality

Let him
Rise above
The cloudy skies
To see the real
Stars

Man
Mustn't admire
The Divine through
False narratives
And flow of
Distortions

Let him
Fight to be free
From the jaws of
Ignorance

Man
Mustn't wait for
Any miracle but
His rational will to
Face the challenge
Head-on...

Deadly
Burst

**When
Any war
Breaks out
People, dreams
And space is
Obliterated,
Sometime quick
Sometime at a
Snail speed**

**War
What a shocker
To humanity
All in all**

**War
What a death of
A civilization
In no time**

**War
What a deep scar
To the unprepared
Beloved beings
All over...**

Beware

Let's
Keep eyes
Open
If the enemy
Tricked us into
A sneaky but fatal
Germ warfare

Time
To be on alert
For the enemy is
Very cunning and
Got long time
Experience

Let's
Be alert and
Keep our eyes
Open for the
Enemy is
Very sneaky
And controls
Many germful
Cities...

Long Haul

Human
Never pure and
Perfect and
So must his
Morality and
Reason

Human fighting
For his social truth
Yet never far from
High pile of greed

Human
Quietly wishing to
Be an ethical will yet
He's under the duress
Of evil deed

Human
Admires what's
Good and true yet
He refuses to let go
His old violent trait

Alas,
It's been a long
Haul to the Temple
Named,
"Sincerity, Honesty
And Authenticity..."

It's All
In the Head

It's
Alright to lose a
Game or two
It's alright to get
Hurt in a relation
Once in a while

I say,
It's okay to be
A victim in a
Failed mission
So long,
If you don't
Quit the scene

That's
Life and
That's
The learning
Adventure
To face with
Courage and
I say with some
Good laugh...

A Wish

Whenever
An ideal and
Rebel joins hands,
Victory waits
By the gate

An ideal seeks
Civility to prevail
A rebel asks to
Change the social
Set-up for good

What if
Such meeting
Of two tales
Helps to
Regain moral
Confidence and
All differences to
Vanish from the
Troubled scene

Let
Ideals and
Rebels
Confess their
Follies whence
No regret to
Report anymore...

Reckoning

While
Witnessing
Two tales of
One life:
Good and evil
Side by side
A boy grew up
So soon

As a
Fully grown
He kept battling
To secure his place
In a world where
All is measured
By money and
Materiality but
Not the inner
Moral worth

He thought,
"It was
Time to be free
From the corrupt
Cage he was
Trapped in it..."

Flame

While the
Body being
Cremated
His soul
Stood by
To express
Gratitude

While the
Flames kept
Reaching out
To the cosmic
Realm
The soul
Stood close by

To bid,
"Goodbye"
To the human
Who once lived
And dream big...

Soliloquy

"I an
Ordinary
Human...I an artist
Born to paint an
Incredible portrait of
My humanity on this
Canvas named,
Beauty & Truth

"Am a
Creative force
Born
To bring out the
Best from my
Inner core"

"Am also
A struggling
Soul fighting to
To make sense of
My existence so
Children shall
Smile
And sleep well
Nights after nights"

Final
Deal

We
Know so well
The world spins
Around with myriad
Subjective opinions
And there's a
Dust storm going
On every where

Oh yes,
There is
That cacophony
Deafening
Humanity every
Now and then and
There's a thick fog
Hanging over
His head

Time to
Reframe
Time to change

Time to
Be silent before
Taking the next step...

A Pause

Yet
Endless cycles
Of
Comings and
Goings keeps
The scenery
Beautiful and
So deceptively
Unchanged

All- That-Is
Evolving
Something into
Better than
What it is

Let the
Notion be
Grasped
Within the
Great Sphere
Called:
Reason
But never a
Blind faith...

King Fear

When
Primitive humans
Experienced
Mighty forces of
Nature
A supernatural
Being was born in
Their fearful minds

That's where
Superstitions and
Myths took
Hold and later
The seed of fear
Seized by the
Institutionalized
Clever few

As bells of
Man-made
Glory of God
Rang
Louder...world
Kept wounding
Wounding
Time after time

As morality and
Reason waned
Humanity
Turned to the
Divided tribes of
Myopia and phobia
In the end...

Nobles

When
Darkness
Engulfs
Unprepared
World
There emerges
A monster:
Fear and Greed

At
That point,
Hope begins
To flee and folks
Come under
The grip of
Nagging despair

In such a
Gloom and doom
Place
Only Unbounded
Heroes shall
Care to fight with
Calm and cool...

Modern
Woman

Modern
Woman who's
Self-confident,
So refined and
Standing tall
For her dignity
At all time

Modern
Woman an
Emerging force
To be reckoned
From this time on

Make
No mistake
She's a fire ball
Illuminating her
Self-respect before
Deaf realm of men

Modern
Woman an
Incredible power
Challenging the
World
At this moment...

Dilemma

Mind
Intricately
Woven between
Unconscious
Wishes and outer
Social façade

If
Hidden wishes
Nakedly Spills
Over the
Social grid,
He's branded,
'Insane' or
Locked-up
For sometime

If
Stuck with
His
Social constraints
He may lose
Freewill
To gain deep
Insight!

Love

When lovers
Fall into the old trap
Of cruel jealousy and
Infidelity
All hell breaks lose
And there is nothing
Left but the emotional
Stress taking two souls
To their waiting graves

When lovers
Fall into the state of
Deceptive ways to
Survive
Trust is gone
And there is nothing
Left but their shattered
Old dreams to die

Love is
Not what one
Thinks or dreams,
It's an iron-clad
Sacred vows
Between two souls
To trust and to
Respect at all time...

Mind Above

Let's not
Live
Momentarily
Let's go
After eternity

Let's not
Rot in evil
Let's
Leave the
Cave
Immediately

Let's
Drop
Arrogance
Let's
Embrace
Goodness

Let's not
Waste time
Over bickering
Trivial things

Let's
Enjoy
Lyrics, rhythms
And meaning of
All –That- Is
We wish to adore...

Off the
Box

Don't think
Life is absurd
That's the
Loser's claim

Albeit
Life is worth for
There's a hidden
Purpose yet to
Emerge on the scene

Got to drop
False narratives:
Pessimism, skepticism,
Nihilism and
Face life as it is

Time
To roll-up
The sleeves to
Shape the future
For our kids and
Theirs to come

Lets
Hurry before
We miss the train
Loaded with
Lots of enthusiasm
And determined will...

Grand
View

It's the
Grand window
That opens to
See what life
Ought to be

It's
A perfect scene
From a
Magic point of
View

Yes
To be
A creative
Pulse of the
Whole

Let's
Just glance
Reality through
This wide window
Offering us
A grand view...

Revelation

Take a bow
With calm
Aim and
Shoot the
Arrow right
Into the
Bull's eye

Take a deep
Breathe and
Stand tall with a
Determined will and
Shoot through the
Deep shaft to meet
The Self for the
First time...

Soldiers
On March

Hey girls
Don't you worry
We'll return home
Soon to sing with
You again

Hey girls
We're on our
Way to fight the
Enemy to bring
Peace to the
Waiting world

Hey, girls
We love you
Too and we'll
See you soon

Hey lovely
Sweet girls don't
Drop tears we'll
Be home soon

Yes
We'll be home
Soon...yes, yes we'll
Be kissing you again
For we love you so deep...

Discovery

What
An incredible
Journey

Let it
Roll along
With wonders
After wonders

Let it
Glow with
New experience
After experience

That's
The miracle of
Human to be

That's the
Magic of
Love and a sweet
Song of our souls...

Up and
At 'em

When
Stars are no
Longer so bright
And no mad-winds
Bringing fresh
Air from the mighty
Blue Seas

In such
A sterile place
Let us be doubly
Determined to
Clear the
Grey clouds of
Our day

Let courage
Be test of our
Collective will
To fight the evil
Head on

Time
To cleanse our
Corrupt minds
Time
To regenerate
Moral strength
To clear
The hanging
Grey clouds...

Profile

Life
What a moving
Painting of
Opinions, visions
And ever changing
Scenarios
Stretching between
Birth and death

But the painting
Is never complete
For the canvas keeps
Expanding; bringing
Chaos and divisional
Strife on the scene

Life though
Complex still
So simple and elegant
But the profile on the
Canvas fails to convey
The real message indeed...

Let it
Spark!

**Every being
Is a growing
Image
In the mirror of
Thoughts, words
And deeds**

**He ain't
Ordinary but
A special breed
Born to make
Some difference**

**Every being
Is a gift of reason
Toward good**

**Let him
Be an
Illumined spark
What
He has been,
Always...**

God
Be Willing!

**In their final
Hallucination
Folks believed
So sincerely,
"They shall be
Free if accepted
The will of the
Almighty"**

**Instead, the
Dear Lord
Insisted:**

*Not
My will but
Through your
Moral will
Show me you're
Free from violence
And senseless killing
Which you've been
Conducting in my
Good name*

**The issue:
Why not meet
Almighty's
Demand, if
We adore Him
So much!**

Flash

Existence
Is in flux
Where
Good and evil
Intermingled
Always

Ever since
The worlds
Been suspended
Into
Conflicting opines,
Subjectivity and
Tribal mindset;
Hope seems to
Eclipsed from
The blessed scene

A few
Wise men
Rejected
World of ignorance
Even they knew their
Death was imminent
But their truth prevailed

Let us draw
Inspiration from those
Awakened souls who
Stood firm
To build a better
World....

Let's
March

Let's
March
Together
To reach the
Mountain high
On time

Let's
Band together
To meet the
Waiting dream
At the highest
Peak of all

Its
Relevant
We know
The realm while
Walking
Through its
Every nightmare

Let's
March together
For the terrain is
So rough and tough,
But we're no less...

Point
North

Don't
You wish
Spirit of hope
Stays forever

Don't
You wish
The endless
Cycles of evil
Breaks off
Soon

Don't
You wish
Worlds
Free from
False
Godly claims

Don't
You think
Let rational
Goodwill
Dictate our lives
For a change!

Prolong
Dialogue

Existence
Seems
A prolonged
Waiting game

It's a
Generational
And never ends
And still
No answer to his
Pressing quest

Existence
What a
Protracted
Dialogue of
Awakened
Minds

Sorry
There are
No listeners in
The Audience!

New
Dawn

For
Too long
The world
Remained in
Interpretative
Possibilities;
Failing to grasp
What's the
Meaning of his
Moral being

Meanwhile
Sanctimonious
Servants
Guided the ship,
But detoured
It from true
Meaning
Off and on

Time to rethink
Time to redefine
Human being not
Tomorrow but today
Here and now....

Not Right

On this
Earthly
Paradise
Just take a
Look:

Inhabitants
Are wrapped by
Million frictional
States of mind

No wonder
History's been
Written mostly
In red ink

O
The notion of
'Earthly paradise'
What a
Crazy whim
To think!

Wisdom

Faith with
Reason is
Verily an
Asset in
True sense

Belief
Powered by
False narratives
Got no chance

For it
Shall die
Under its
Irrational
Weight

When
Enlightenment
Emerges as the
Dominant
Experience

We
Must accept it,
Adapt it
To end the
Long ignorance...

Power

Let the
Core of
Every being
Be a
Dynamo
Generating
Endless courage
On the scene

Let every
Being be the
Center of
Good always

And let him
Spill over
Ethical will to
Triumph in the
End

I ask,
"Why not be
The heroes of
Our time when
All attributes are
Already installed
In us!"

Ringing
Bells

In
The end
We're
All going to
Die and no
Surprise there

Before
Our times up,
Let courage and
Rational goodwill
Ford us to the shore

Let us
Also arrive
At a point of
Reckoning:

"Our deeds
Govern
Consequences thus
Our destiny as well."

Unity

Human
Roaming through
This panorama
Yes, through this
Vast and colorful
Universe

He's
Awed by its
Splendor yet
Fails to know
He is a part of
Mesmerizing
Magic too

Why then
Chase after
Perfection
When he's
Already!

Let him
Leave the cave
Let him
Know there is
Sun shine,
Bright skies and
Blue seas waiting to
Link him with the
Vast Universe...

Stubborn

Lovers living
In the world of
Fantasy
Often fall onto
A wrong Track

They
Keep going in
Circles from
Attraction to
Friction
Then separation
And back again if
Lucky

Love
Demands
Discipline, trust
And wisdom

Love
Demands
Forgiveness and
Good sense of
Humor

If you
Own 'em, you're
Indeed winner of
Your
Budding romance...

Storm

We're pulses
Of life rolling
Along
The wonders of
This expanding
Universe

Struggles and
Challenges make
Us stronger than
What
We're before

We got to
Evolve from
Innocence to
Awakening for
That's our mission

That's the
Essence of our
Journey we're on

That's
The noble goal
We must aim to
Attain
Before time is no
Longer our friend...

La La
Land

When
Humans
Succumb to
The old illusion
Of their belief
That's where
Their trouble
Begins

Today,
Smart robotics
Are threatening
Holy
Self-respect and
Honor of the
World citizens

And sadly
Still humans think
New reality shall
Be okay with 'em

An old illusion
Thrives best when
Truth is ignored
And consequences
Hit upon us like
Death nails on a
Waiting coffin...

Last
Letter

Soon
I'll be home
To kiss you dear
Heart

But let me
Get through
Tonight for the
Enemy is strong and
Hiding all around

I'm
Alert at all time
But
You know dear
Life's not a
Guaranteed
In any war zone

If I am
Unable to see
You again
Just know,
"I've always
Loved you so
Deep with all
Sincerity of
My heart"

I remain your
Soul forever

Heroes
Forever

Damn right
Our lives matter
The most and
It mustn't be
Reduced
To nothing by
Anyone and
Anywhere
In the world

We're
All heroes
For we're the
Awareness,
"Who we're"

We're
Heroes and we
Mustn't budge
Today or tomorrow
Anymore

We're
All heroes here
To build a better
World

Damn right
We're
All heroes for
We never die for
Our noble cause...

Fading
Vows

Don't say,
We never had a
Lovely time

Don't
Even say,
We never came
Close together

Don't say,
We never loved
Good enough

I ask,
"Don't live in the
World of denial"

Do you
Know,
Love asks
Not to run away

Dear lady,
Love is honesty
And mutual trust
Not jealousy and
Selfish convenience...

Spirit

In reality,
Human is his
Metaphysical
Journey

That keeps
Him evolving
Toward
Enlightenment

Human
What an
Upward
Moving story
Since the very
Beginning

He's been
Contradictory
Many times...even
Ruthless at times
All in all
He keeps spinning
On the Great Wheel
To meet his
Metaphysical twin...

Freedom

Be free to
Roam this
Magnifique
Realm for
We're the
Children of the
Cosmic mom

Just
Get off
Man-made
Constraints:
And
Reach out to
The unity of all

Get on the
Road to freedom
Where equality of
All souls is already
Written in this
Ever growing...
Ever throbbing
Vast Universe...

Destiny

Conscience
Certainly an
Eternal flame
Of the inner
Spirit

It's
An arrow
Shot through
World of chaos
But still steady
On a path
To the
Right direction

Reason
Too is
An eternal flame
Of hope albeit a
Sharp arrow shot
Through world of
Despair and still
Steady on a path
To the
Right awareness...

Déjà vu

Oh yes,
We're living
In the world of
'Glorified illusion'
Today

We're
Turning to be
Citizens of the
Great Lost land
With our highly
Addicted
Techno spirit
Alright

Tacitly,
We're reduced
To be consumer-
Slaves and
Our worth is
Nothing more than
Raw data to be mined

It's
The Orwellian
Control of thoughts
To bend our wills

Candidly,
It's the same old
Game we call it now,
"Tech-slavery, that's all!"

Fly
Beyond

As we keep
Going through
The Storm
We don't know
Where shall we
End-up

As we keep
Rolling through
The nagging
Uncertainty
We don't know
If all dreams shall
Vanish or what

In such a
Tenuous situation
Let us
Reverberate
The world:
We're
Born to be
Heroes of our time
We're strong and
We're free to go on...

Awakened

What's
The point
Being a fatigue
Spirit and
Despaired
Mindset

What's
The reward
While
Bickering and
Fighting for asinne
Tribal claims

Time to
Break off the
Chain imposed
On our wills

Yes,
Let's erase
The ills of
The world
To end this
Dark charade...

Waves

Life
What a
Capricious
Wave of crests and
Troughs passing
Through thin threads
Of grief and joy

Life
What an
Imperfection of
Obsolete belief and
Irrational claims

At the crest
His golden time
Humanity enjoyed
Its best experience

In trough,
Evil reigned and
Deconstructed
His dream

Life
What a flow of
Highs and lows...rights
And wrongs...births and
Deaths with no good
Explanation 'til the end!

Die Hard

Funny,
At the
Very beginning
All are
Equal in innocence
And curiosity to explore
Their fascinating world
All around

Once born,
We remain pure
Through infancy
And bit more

As we
Turn teens,
We're
Fed by heavy
Doses of
Divided claims:
Religion, race and
All other craps;
Sowing the seed of
Tribal warfares

Once
Caught into
The old habits of
Hatred, violence and
War... we become
Dumb citizens of the
Living hell on Earth!

Quest

What's the
Measure of life
When all is in
Chaotic flux

What's the
Limit of a sphere
When it keeps
Expanding forever

What's the
Set moral
Reference
When we're
Caught into the
Whirlwind of
Violent acts

What's
The meaning of
Existence if we
Fail to
Comprehend
Truth within

What if
All quests are
Just to prove our
Rational superiority
In the end or what!

Curse

My
Mentor once
Said so aptly,

"War
Promotes
Injustice,
Cruelty and
Criminality and
Nothing better
Returns to the
World"

He
Continued,
"War degrades
Humanity and
That's a chilling
Indictment
Throughout
History and sadly
Happening today"

He concluded,
"War is the effect
As it erupts from
The mind of man"

Search

Where
Do we draw
The limit,
Who's
Good and
Who's not

Where do
We
Move from
Here over
There with a
Victory full of
Meaning

When
Do we
Say to the
Corrupt world,
"Enough
Is enough"

Weak-link

In the
Specter of
Mirage,
Bridge
Between
Light & dark
Seems so foggy

Life
Doesn't
Pardon
Struggling
Spirits

Human
What a
Sacred link
Between past
And present
Yet not ready
To tie 'em with
The right future!

Future
Is Today

As world
Keeps spinning
And the
Beats goes on
Let's not
Forget children
Are our future
Indeed

Don't
Let 'em drop
Tear and
Don't let 'em
Live in fear

Be sure
To nourish 'em
With right values
And right vision

Children
Be inspired
For they're the
Destiny of our
Species in the
Entire Universe...

Beware

Don't
Let a drop
Of water be
Lost
For it sustains
The mighty ocean

Don't
Let single grain
Of top soil be
Gone for
It ensures life,
In essence

Don't
Let greed
Get stronger
It robs
Our collective
Moral strength

Don't let
Dogmas and
False piety kill our
Rational goodwill
They make
Existence meaningless...

Expedition

Each an
Individual unit
Who's a part of
A big chain

Each
A builder of
Dream
Life after life
Until colliding
With death
Time after time

Each a
Special creative
Force keeps
Pushing forward
To the North Star

Each an
Intelligent being
Focused on his
Set noble goal
Until colliding with
Million "Nay Sayers"
Time after time...

That's It

Life
Got to be a
Wonderful
Poetic
Experience

Life
Got to be
Swinging with
Motley lyrical
Whims

Life
What a
Inspiring
Overture to
Feel

Life
What a
Change and
Necessity
Of creative
Force to sing...

Fickle

Romance
At times,
Turns into a
Deceptive pleasure
Swinging between
Love and hate

If it
Goes sweetly
Well
Lovers are lucky
To stick around
For a long

If it's
Get sour,
Love takes
One-eighty and
Distrust engulfs
The affair

Oh yes,
Romance
What a heavenly
Experience between
Two lovers either
To remember or
Be thrown into the
Fire and brimstone...

Garden

Why
Haven't the
Clouds dressed
The naked
Skies yet

If and
When
They do,
Will there
Be a
Garden glowing
With zillion
Roses to beautify
The world
We love and
Adore so much!

Locked-on

Let our
Collective spirit
Keep rolling
To get the job
Done in time

Who cares
What others may
Think ...just keep
The spirit going,
Rolling and rolling all
The way to the goal

Let there be
Rain or shine...let's
Fight the challenge
Of our time

Just keep
Going and going
'Til the mission of
Our set dream is
In our hands

I say,
Just keep the
Spirit
Rolling and rolling
'Til we've
Met our moral self...

Mighty
Blue

**Man
Standing by the
Mighty Blue
Sea**

**He was
Thrilled by the
Oncoming
Strong waves
Bringing
Fresh energy to
Cleanse the dirty
Shore for sure**

**Suddenly,
He saw
The mighty Blue
Drowning all his
Contradictions,
Paradoxes and
False beliefs to
The abyss**

**He
Cried with a
Greatest joy,
"Yes...yes
I can bury all
My corrupt point
Of views today too!"**

Sphere of Doubt

Sometimes
I wonder what's
The meaning of this
Endless cycle of
Birth and death

Sometimes,
I also wonder
What if
We don't
Know the truth,
Even we're
Intelligent
And so smart

Sometimes
I keep awake all
Night
To understand
The meaning of
Totality-of-all-
Human experience

Sometimes
I wonder what's the
Glory behind the essence
Of God when humans
Been bleeding for a
Very long!

Epiphany

Death
A dark
Shadow of
Life perhaps

Life
In turn
Plagued by
Seven sins
As always

One day,
Man decided
To fight the
Disease head-on

At that
Instant his
Attitude changed
And he emerged
A moral giant
On the scene

He
Broke through
All barriers of
Yesterday and
Marched on with
A new confidence:
I can climb the
Mighty mountain,
Any time I want...

Time
To Roll

Damn right
We've
Been waiting
Too long

Damn right,
We've
Been asking
To begin the
Noble mission
For a long

Let's
Be one
Mighty force in
This change
And flow

Damn right,
We've been
Aimlessly
Running around
On this highway
For a long...

Half-Baked

How do we
Tackle with
Violence,
Hatred and war
While we're
Half-animal and
Half-human still

We
Tried myths,
Superstitions and
Sang million times,
"Glory to
The merciful
Almighty" but no
Resolution to our
Struggling fate

Sadly
No
Full wisdom
Filling up our
Three pound
Thinking bag yet

Oh yes.
It's human nature
That hasn't changed
And habits of
The past never left
Us free...

Matrix

How
To build
A bridge
Between faith
And reason
Has been a
Serious challenge
Yet to be resolved

How
Do we justify
In relying on
This three pound
Thinking machine
When all riddles
Are trapped into
This expanding
Vast universe

And how
Do we grasp
Enigma of the
Soul that's still
Stranger to us!

Transformation

What if
Very magic
Of bucolic beauty
Transforms a corrupt
City dweller into
Something humble
Indeed

What if
The city fellow
Breathes fresh air and
Dives into crystal waters
Of a simple rural milieu
Will he wash off all his
Big sins!

When
Returning his old
World of
Hypocrisy, glittered
And big social egos

Will he be
Fearful he
May not remain
A tranquil
Rural soul much long!

Flashing
Light

If we've not
Looked for love
Today
It may not come
Again

If we've not
Cared for others
It may haunt always

Let's learn
To extend
Hand of
Friendship with
Not bitterness

Let's learn
To be moral with
A purpose and
Enjoy life as is...

The Flow

River of
Dreams keep
Flowing so slowly
But steadily toward
The mighty Blue Sea

Thirsty
He's for wisdom
While
Walking through
His ticking time

During
Daylight all is
So clear and so
Glorified to his
View

It's
The dark
That upwells
Evil, harming
His noble Soul

But
The river keeps
Flowing with
No concern at all ...

Existence

Adversity
Must be
Hall mark of
Human
Existence

In turn,
Existence
Got the
Signature,
Glorified
Illusion

Such is
The daring
Story of humans
Full of blunders

Funny,
Human
Assumptions
Sinks and swims
And
There is no big
Concern...

Open-up

We Sing
Million prayers
In the name of
Almighty daily

But not
Knowing the
Real message
Is a big sin

In the
Big picture,
Almighty may be
The First Cause
But again
It's for humans
To get the job done

Intelligent
Beings must play
The game well
For its time
To take
Charge to know
The real essence...

Dynamics

Don't know
Where
All shall end
It's
A cat and
Mouse game

I've tried
Hard to know
My world

I've tried
To grow with
The world

I've
Traveled
Million miles
To know
My world

And I've
Yet to grasp
My own world!

Excursion

I've lived to
Seek meaning
Of all that is

I've lived to
Feel truth of
My lady

I've tried to
Guide my kids
To be good

And I know
My journey is
Shortened by the
Minutes

While
I've brief time
Left to say:
"Well hello!"

Bull's
Eye

Don't
Let him
Falter
Don't
Let him
Lie

Don't let
Him buy
False values
Of his time

Let him
Just keep
Evolving
To the
Shining
North Star...

Daring
Journey

**A Child
Is a
Hero
In-making**

**Let's give
Him/her
Best to move
From
Innocence to be
A moral being**

**If they
Grow up to be
Good
So shall the
World**

**Adults
Didn't fair
Well
But children
Are getting ready
To correct their
Foolish old ways...**

Cheers!

We must
Motivate young
Minds today

It's vital
They be inspired
To be better than
"Who they are"

Let the
World reckon
Their awesome
Power

To liberate
Humankind
From follies of
The past

They shall
Shade light to
The dark

Cheers!
Let 'em
Justify their
Noble births...

Consequence

Where
Ignorance reigns
And hubris prevail
That's where moral
Death occurs

Where
Lovers betray
Trust
That's where
Two hearts die
At once

Humans
Designers of
Their truth
Will they
Ever
Find a way to
The Temple of
Good!

Inspire
'Em

Don't
Drown
'Em
Into
Myopic
World of
Old ideas

Don't
Let 'em
Fall into the
Jaws of
Deceptive tales

Don't
Let them
Touch hell

Let 'em
Inspire,
How to be a
Good human
'Til the end...

A Glimpse

What if
God said:
I am giving you this
Supreme power of reason
To explore my mind, so
Use it well with your
Moral intention

Humans replied,
"Alright Lord as
You wish"

Lord reminded:
Be sure to ignore
Intermediaries
They're
There to save
Their selfish needs
In my good name

In time,
Humans forgot
Lord's guidance
And got
Tangled into
False narratives,
Pseudo-worships
And jingoistic frenzy

What a
Sad history
To recall in this
Terrific
Twenty-first century!

Great Day

What a
Great way to
Laugh and love
Today

What a
Glorious way
To march toward
Mountain top
Today

Let's
Sing and dance
For we're alive
Everyday

Let's just
Meet and hug
Every
Happy face,
Today...

Profile

We adore
Celebrities,
And big stars
For their
Talents alright

Remember
They're
Enlarged celluloid
Images flashed
On a mega-
Digital screens

We
Worship
The mighty One
Of course with
Full devotion
Since we hold
His magnified
Image
Cropped up by
Million glorified
Themes

In reality,
We
Must rely on
Our rational
Goodwill and
Endeavor to
To realize our
Noble purpose,
Simply...

Beautiful
Seed

Neither
Men's
Connection
With Divinity
Nor to
The society but
To himself first

If the
Unit is strong
So shall be the
Whole

If the
Seed is good
So shall be the
Big garden of
Hope

Let
Billion flowers
Bloom and
Let 'em turned
Astoundingly
Inspiring
Venue...

Reality
As Is

This vast
Throbbing
Universe seems
Driven-by
An unknown
Essence

From
Birth to death
All is going from
Dark to light,
Wrong to right
Evil to good;
Spinning on
Their own

In such
A dynamic flux
Reality seems
Elusive...so deceptive
And yet so inspiring
At the same time...

Twins

Since life
Swings
Sometime high
And at times low;
Living between
Reality and
Fantasy is
A big struggle
To hold-on

Fantasy
Brings free
Flow of feelings
Of many dreams

But the
Societal
Restraints
Shackles freewill

Life
Always a
Wonderful
Double
Experience
Never giving
Full perfection...

Avoir

Da, da...da, da
....da, dad...da
One two three
Darling let's say,
"Goodbye today"

Let's
Just be free from
Promises we
Vowed yesterday

Da, da...da, da
....da, da...da
Darling
Let's count one
Two three before
We go crazy with
Daily debates

Da, da...da, da
....da, da...da
One two three
Dear lady
Let's be free to
Flee our ways
Today

Da, da...da, da
....da, da...da
Dear O dear lady
I say one two three
Let's just kiss and
Bid, 'Avoir' 'til we
Never meet again...

A Note

Just a note
To the 'pious
Self-righteous' who
Thinks they're nearer
To the Almighty than
Others who pray
Differently

This
Is a also a
Reminder
Yes, to the
Wealthy
Who tacitly
Think
They're better
Than most others

It's
A brief note
To the hi-tech
Big boys who
Hold they can steal
Privacy of all beings
And can bring
'Em to their knees...

Be
Bold

When
A promise is
Subjective
And incoherent

Its
Conclusion
Ensues chaos and
Humanity goes
Into tail spin of
Confusion

Don't
Give up
But be bold
And
Don't let the
Guards down

We're
Rational beings
Born to clarify
All
That is unknown...

Double
Dealer

**Human
What a
Complex social
Creature stirred by
Million whims**

**His
Outer shell
Hides all
Dionysian habits
And crazy feelings**

**In
Dream he's
Honest with his
Unfulfilled wish
In
Reality he's a
Different being**

**What a
Magic is
Human nature
Who keeps
Walking through
The royal road of
"Double Deals"**

Lovely
Lady

Hey my
Lovely lady
Don't look down
Upon me for
'Am an honorable
Fellow and won't
Take your
Insults anymore

Yes
My proud lady
You can't bend my
Dignity and honor
For your pleasures
Anymore

I say,
My lovely lady
Time to drop envy
Time
To grow up and
Accept your folly

Hey my
Good lady,
The world keeps
Spinning daily and
Doesn't care how
High you think
You may be!

Our
Time

Even when
Light keeps
Darkness
Away

Folks
Keep asking,
"Where's the
Illuminated
Road?"

When life
Is filled with
Hope and
Happiness
And folks
Still
Keep asking,
"Why ain't
Good times
Here?"

Seems they
Forgot to ask,
"Is there
Hero in 'em
Who's willing to
Open their eyes?"

Where's
He

Am
Thinking,
How to
Go back in time
And correct the
Errors of the past

Often,
'Am amazed
By the gifted
Beings
Who
Still wonder

Why do
They always
Fall short of
Reaching
Their set goal!

Too Late!

At
Very top
Of
Awakening

A man
Began to scan
His own
Life and time

And
Understood
All was
Ephemeral and
Could vaporize
At anytime

He
Was once
Under a
Heavy load
Of arrogance
And
Disowning his
Humanity as well

But then
He was
A dying man
Wishing to be a
Better next time!

First
Step

We
Shall come
To our
Common sense
When
Thrown onto the
Road to nowhere

We
Shall be
Willing to
Look for light
When
Dropped into a
Dark cave for
A very long

We shall
Learn
How to take
The first step
When
We regain our
Courage and
Moral will which
May take a long time...

Scar

One
Wrong thought
One
Untimely word
One
Terrible act

Can
Transform
Our
Gentle person
Into an evil
Event in no time

Remember
Slavery,
Violence
Wars even
Genocides left
Deep scars in the
Conscience of all
Good folks forever

In the end
We're the
Sole owners of
Experience,
Perception...
Judgment and
We ink the history
As well...

We're
The Story

They write
Plays and
Make mega-films
To tell the story of
Human in myriad
Ways

Always in each
Story there is
Eternal friction
Between
"Good & Evil"

After
Over coming
Many obstacles ,
Protagonist triumphs
In end most always

At times,
Viewers
Fail to grasp
That there's
A tacit message:
To stay with
The side of light
For darkness
Yields nothing but
An ignominious
Defeat in the end...

Unity
Indeed

Let
Real and ideal
Join hands to clarify
How life ought to be

First:
To be
A disciplined
Mind

Second:
To be
Hopeful

Third:
To be
One vision,
"How they
Ought to be!"

Pacifica

Pacific
The biggest,
The
Deepest and
What a
Magnificent
Ocean Blue
On Planet Earth

So
Wonderfully
Named,
"Peaceful"
What a
Solace to the
World indeed

Never forget
This mighty
Blue tranquility
Rides on a
Deadly tectonic
Fury beneath...

Here
We're

In the
Big picture
Of reality

Irony of
Human not
In divinity, but
In his overly
Glorified
Belief

Irony
Not in
Devotion of
Almighty, but
In his sheer
Ignorance
Indeed

Irony
Not of an
Unknown cause,
But in failing
To regenerate
Goodwill in the
World...

Omnipotent

Man
Got the power
To be
Larger than
Life

If he's
Determined
To attain
The set goal

Man can
Kiss distant
Stars if
He grasped
His set mission
On time

Man can
Lift humanity
Sky high if
He reaches
Clarity, poignancy
And integrity
Of mind...

Our
Tale

We're
An imperfect
State of mind
Fighting so hard
To make it alright

For a brief
We thrived with
Reason and deep
Insight and we
Called it,
"Golden Age"

Alas
For a long
Evil choices
Kept corrupting
Our world and
We
Became citizens
Of a
"Sheer hell!"

Nova

Let's
Begin with a
New vision:

A is for
Admiration
Of humanity

B is for
Beauty within

C is for
Concern for
Planet itself

Let
ABC be the
Flashing light
Guiding us
Through
The stygian
Night...

An Image

What if
Super-intelligent
Aliens conducted
An experiment on
Earthlings

What if
They realized,
These semi-animals
Though possess
Great ideals
Yet unable to
Perform well for
Some odd reason

"Wait!" said one
Of the aliens with
Alacrity,
"Earthlings got
Conscience above
Their shortcomings"

Their leader
Observed,
"Earthlings
Got good future
If they
Could wake-up
From their
Long slumber."

A Snap

Let young
Be aware:
Existence can
Snap like a thin
Thread if not
Governed well

It's
Equally true
If love and hope
Are ignored for
A long

All things
Would snap in
A Nano sec too

Pent-up
Stress is a
Dangerous
Nemesis

Be sure to
Handled it with
An inner care,
Wisdom and
Common sense...

Tossed
Dice

Love
Brings
Two lonely
Hearts together
To be one forever

And
There begins
Their journey
With
Consequences
To bear always

If all is well,
It's a splendid
Experience all the
Way to heavenly
Dream come true

If not,
Their world turns
Into one lasting
Nightmare and hurt
Feelings can't even
Fill their deep
Wounds...

Reflection

The
Issue:

"Why
Don't we
Learn
To live in a
World we
All want?"

The
Riddle:
"Why don't
We
Think ahead
The future
Of our kids?"

The
Tragedy:

"Why
Can't our
Rational minds
Cleanse
The thick fog of
Ignorance!"

Echoes

"Attention,
Attention"

A mysterious
Voice from a
Distant edge of
The Universe
Woke up the
Sleepy world
Of humans

The voice
Reverberated
The azure skies:
Change the
Path you're on, or
You won't survive
Anymore

Sorry the
Super-intelligent
Beings
Didn't realize
They were talking
To a deaf world...

Lost

Don't say
It's
Sad world
We live in

Don't say
It's
Dark forever

No point
Sinking into
Double despair

Don't say
It's
Worst time
We're in

Don't
Ignore but
Know

How to
Stop the
Recurring
Blunders...

Assessment

We're
Winners
Every where
And every time

Damn right
We're
Born to win
Every game
Every time

Yes,
We're
What we are
We fight the
Enemy
Anywhere
We want

We're
Eternal
We see glass full
But never half
Yes,
That's who we are
Damn right we're
Winners at all time...

The
Saga

And look at
Either historic
Or present time
Human
In collision with
War and peace,
Love and hate
Pleasure and pain

His life
Seems filled with
Complex tale of
Suffering and
Not much gain

Beware:
He may not
Go any higher
If his soul stays
Tangled with
Two opposing
Forces of existence...

Real
Being

An
Inspiring
Thought
Got to be a
Rational
Goodwill

A Noble
Point of view
Got to be a
Determined
Will to win

It's via
Metaphysical
Journey
He's the real
Moral Soul
Who emerges on
The blessed scene...

A View

One
Can be
A humble and
Meek and
Can turn
Larger than life

He has
Power
To inspire
Generations for
Their noble aim

It's
Not the
Pretty looks and
Sweet talks that
Yield solace
It's
Simple kindness
Can lift humans
To the highest
Mountain peak...

Ennui

Modern
Man
Who's
In love with
Magic of the
Techno-spell

Not knowing
So well what
May be its
Consequence

Modern
Man still
Keeps his
Head into
The sand
Not knowing
The tide is on

He may not
Escape
If he doesn't get
Off the mesmerized
Techno spell in time...

Duty Call

Where
Intricate
Relationship
Exists and
Where
Justice prevails
That's the world
We all wish to
Live in

Where
Reason prevails
Where
Humans are
Dignified

That's
The realm
We all
Want to be in

Where
Children feels
Safe and can
Dream that's
The future
We must make it
Happen in our time...

Edge

What if
Death
Strikes a
Human
Sooner than
He thinks

What if
Death
Awakens
His soul
For a change

What if
Residual hope
Leaps higher
Than ever

Will man
Conquor the
Fear of death?

Naked

A man took
A nose dive into
Sacred waters of
Lake
"Inspiration"

And
Emerged naked
As all his sins
Were washed
Away

He stood
Tall by the shore
And declared
To the world:

I am
The holder of
My destiny
I am
The owner of
My long journey

As naked
Am I with
My truth today
I know how to
Navigate through
The dirty waters of
Life after life and got
No complain to report...

Being
She is

**After
A long
Contemplation
She got up and
Informed the
World:**

**Nothing
To show
Nothing
To prove but
The courage
I hold**

**Nothing
So new
Nothing to view
But the confidence
I hold**

**Nothing
To be
Concerned
Nothing
To be
Feared but to
Complete journey
Of my Soul...**

History
Singing

It's an
Aphrodisiac
Power of war
That gave birth to
Human glory and
Tragedy
At the same time

Human
Never quits from
The jaws of arrogant
Ambitions to rule
The weak

He
Even imposed
His tribal will
On others to
Worship his
Claimed brand
Of belief

Well many
Kings, emperors
And petite rulers
Came and gone
Leaving nothing
But their left over
Eroding ruins,
Atrocious deeds
To be scorned
By the livings...

Cosmic
Seeds

Let's inspire
Children with
These few words:

Human
Is a unique
Gift for he has
Power to illuminate
Every soul

Human
Is incredible
For he has
Strength to rid off
Evil in an instant

Human
Is indeed
A live courage in
Action for he can
Fire-up all young
Braves

Human
Is an eternal
Hope for he can lift
All collective hopes...

Aimless

He ain't
Going
Anywhere
But to be here
For a brief

Alone
There is a
Fusion of life
And death
In him

Alone
He can be
Formidable
And who
Can't be
Ignored

In the end,
Mustn't he
Correct all
Egregious choices
He made!

Rage

A man
Walking along
The perfidious
Road

Thought he's
Ready to settle
The old score

While lost
In the grip of
Blind rage
He forgot he is
Equally guilty in
Conflict on-hand

Revenge
What
A powerful
Aphrodisiac;
Turning
Human to be
A killer
Animal in an
Instant...

Here & Now

What a
Metaphysical
Experience of
Man from
Vagueness to
Abstraction

Life
What a
Continuum
Meditation
To be born as a
Spiritual Being

In the
Big picture,
Death must be
A special event
Beyond

Where
New journey
Begins perhaps
With a
Renewed meaning
All we know!

Roar

While
Caught by
The fury of his
Emotional stress
A man was ready
To break free
From his obsolete
Imposed belief

He sought
Freewill
To abandon
Fear within and
Can't wait to
Reset his mission
Before it too late

In his
Desperation
He roared:

I'm
Determined
To be free and
Let me earn my
Rational vision
From now-on to be
Happy once again...

Worms

Some
Try hard to
Claim
Their special
Status
In the society

As they
Love to
Thrive into
A make-belief
Sphere called:
*Money, power
And fame*

Who
Knows
How happy
They may be
While billions
Remain in pain

Who
Knows if
They're
Fearful worms
Crawling into
The dark cave
Called, *Greed!*

Liberty & Necessity

In this
Ever revolving
Grand drama
Of existence

What
Happens when
Moral will of many
Collides against
Few who control
The game

Moralists
Must be
Fearless and
Driven by the
Ethical will
Demanding
Their legal claims

What
An on-going
Battle between,
'David vs Goliath'
In the world where
We value equality and
Dignity of all...

Real

Its time
To erase old
Societal myth

Let him
Handle
His freedom
With a good
Sense of moral
Intention

Alone he's
Prone to
Go wrong
In his
Presumption

Let
The collective
Wisdom bring
Unity of purpose
And that's the
Way to win the
Mission

Freedom
Must mean
Cooperating toward
Common good of all...

Empty
Heads

Virtue
Never in the
Dominion of
Violence, bigotry
And crazy whims

Morality
Never a pulse
Of greedy, selfish
And narcissistic
Beings

Reason
Never a friend of
Anger, revenge
And jealousy to
Say the least

Soul
Never alive
In the world of
Cruelty and
Insane ideologies
Driven by impulsive
Crazy whims...

We
Shall

It's
Clear to me
Life is
Profoundly
Ambiguous filled
With struggling
Traits of many

In such
Total turmoil
Let's
Converge all
Our strengths
For something
To be great

Let's take
The first step
To renew our
Collective
Courage & hope
And then meet
The challenge
Face to face...

Nutshell

Religion
May express
Symbols and
Metaphors, but
Individual is a
High emotional
Intensity in life

He
Demands
Real
Experience,
Reason and
Moral strength

He rejects
False belief
That kept him
Into the
Glorious illusion
Through many
Different ways...

Measure

It was a
Solemn moment
Underway
As the last rites were
Conducted in a village
Named, "Anywhere"

Human
Corpse lay peacefully
On top of a pile of woods
Ready to be cremated

Chief priest
Lit the fire and
Began chanting:

You're
Leaving behind
Knowledge and
Creative acts
But you do carry
All the good deeds

He then
Eulogized:

We've
Gathered here to
Express our gratitude
For what a good
Human you were...

Endurance

Time
After time
Life caught by the
Swirling...spinning
Recurring fire of
Deadly seven sins

Only
Rational
Strength,
Moral depth
And
Determined will
Shall help us
Escape the cage

Before
We die of
Our collective
Failures

Let's
Make it up
With our left over
Care and vision
Atleast for the good
Of our kids... though
It may be too late!

Be in
Control

Of course
It matters for
Human to be the
Owner of his/her
Courage, dignity
And a will to live
Well

It's
For him
To be
Disciplined
And be a
Rational goodwill

Only
Human of such
Caliber shall
Decide the
Outcome of
His mission, his
Life...his destiny
Until the final
Curtain drops...

On the Go

Human
Journey
Begins with
Innocence and
Moves forward
Through
Experience and
Reason

Arriving
At a
Vision where
He
Aspires to be one
"Global Spirit"

It's
The issue of
Will to live well
It's
The matter of
Courage to come
Alive

Let the
Journey reveal
His perfection
That he never
Knew
So well before...

Life

Life
What a
Wonderful
Mystical appeal
May be
A spiritual will
To be worthy of
Being something

Life
What a
Metaphysical
Curiosity to
Explore beyond
The barriers of
'Do's and don'ts'

Life
What a
Incredible
Test between
Good and evil

Life
What a
Vacillating
State of mind
Where friction is
Also the experience

Life
What a splendor
Full of vigor, rhythm
And lyrics to sing ...

Pursuit

No point
Dwelling into
This crazy,
'Mental illusion'
For there ain't
Good return

No point
Pursuing
Blind belief
For there ain't
Good answer
In return

Why not
Drop the
Distortion and
Move on with a
Right vision...

Headlines

Grand
Saga of
Humans
Seems all
About fatalistic
Confrontation
With death

It's been
Tough-of-war
Between
'Us and them'
"Hate and love"
While
Denying
Durable peace
On the battlefield

Why not
Regain our
Original gift of
Courage and calm
To beat the challenge
Of our time!

Mirror

On looking
Through the
Shattered mirror
Of existence

Human
Unable to free
From blatant
Hypocrisy
Of his time

What if
He cleanses
His fuzzy mind
And takes an
Another glance

Will
He ever
See in it
Societal unity
Rolling along with
A right vision!

Fortitude

Life
At times
Turns into
An issue of
Personal
Culpability
Albeit an
Individual
Conscience
To bear with it

In such
Strings of
Recurring
Experience
His
Inner strength
Must endure

Also in
Such a
Stiff struggle of
Thick and thin
He must guard
His honor, dignity
And the future of
His kids...

Witness

What if
Human is
No more than
An abstraction,
Adaptation and
Rearrangement of
Ephemeral opinions

Looking
Through the
Lenses of wise men
Everything is in flux
And no guarantees to
Expect any time soon

In the big
Picture of reality,
On seeing
Children at play

I witness
Their
Pure innocence
Dancing
Cheek to cheek with
Freedom but sadly it
Shall pass in time too...

Let's
Grasp

No human be
Overwhelmed by
Recurring tragic
Emotions of pity,
Fear or insecurity
Now on

It be
Understood,
Existence is a test
Ground where every
Human is measured
By his/her total deeds

Man seems
Disengaged from nature
And the disappointment
Prevail over his choices

In such a
State of imbroglio:
Between light & dark,
Between right & wrong
Between life & death
Let an
Unbounded hero
Emerge on the scene...

Be
Embolden

Immersion
Into the old
Unworkable notions
Be dropped to see
The meaning of the
World as clearly as
We must

No point
In going back to
Habits of dogma
And myopia

No point in
Regretting what
Went wrong before
For we're not there

Let
The invasion of
New ideas and
Open-mindness
Energized our
New
Global vision...

Gist

As we
Begin to
Understand
Death
Purifies life
In the end

Let's get
Busy to erase
Our insane
Tribal traits

As we begin
To understand
Something of
History

Lets
Wake-up to
Our inner sense
Of unity at this
Critical time...

Truth
We Must

**Let's not
Undermine our
Inner strength**

**To seek
A universal
Validity of our
Moral integrity
And rational
Goodwill**

**Let's
Not give-up
Our collective
Hope and
Will to win...**

Glorious
Blunders

When
We got the
Nuke-toys
It was a Faustian
Deal alright

When we
Opened
Democracy to
A cunning foe,
We ended up with
Frankenstein
In return

When we
Preached
Peace and love
To the cultists, we
Ended-up holding
Three thou dead
At the Twin Towers

When
We thought
AI's shall give us
Good life
We seems to
Losing our privacy
And dignity in return!

Renewal

Reflective
Wisdom that's
What we must
Be after

That's
The flashing
Light taking us away
From the dark cavern

Life
Often turns into
An artistic challenge
May be an intellectual
Turmoil or just a social
Struggle

Only moral
Pursuit with
Rational will
Shall save us in
The end

That's the
Reflective wisdom
And not a
Reconciliation,
Anymore...

Devolution

When
Evil and good
Come face to face
Bells of big trouble
Rings louder
By the minutes

When
Two foes
Collide on the
Battlefield
Neither wants to
Back off and the
Danger builds up
By the minutes

As drums of
War keeps louder
Civility burns faster

Anger and
Revenge
Are on fire and
Destruction is
Imminent in such a
Man-made craze...

That
Art Thou

Let's welcome
The Unbounded
Hero of all time
Who's
An irresistible
Force on the go

He can't be contained
He can't be restrained
He's a smasher of all
Obsolete "isms"

Let's welcome
The noble hero who's
A determined will to
Win the challenge of
His time

He's
Not afraid of
Tribal
Jingoistic mindset
He's
Never afraid of
Death

Let's welcome
The noble hero for
He's a future vision
He's a hope forever
Let him awaken our
Slumbering souls...

Recent Books by J.J. Bhatt

(Available from Amazon/Kindle)

HUMAN ENDEAVOR: *Essence & Mission/ a Call for Global Awakening,* **(2011).**

ROLLING SPIRITS: *Being Becoming /a Trilogy,* **(2012).**

ODYSSEY OF THE DAMNED: *A Revolving Destiny,* **(2013).**

PARISHRAM: *Journey of the Human Spirits,* **(2014).**

TRIUMPH OF THE BOLD: *A Poetic Reality, (2015).*

THEATER OF WISDOM, *(2016).*

MAGNIFICENT QUEST: *Life, Death & Eternity, (2016).*

ESSENCE OF INDIA: *A Comprehensive Perspective, (2016).*

ESSENCE OF CHINA: *Challenges & Possibilities, (2016).*

BEING & MORAL PERSUASION: *A Bolt of Inspiration, (2017).*

REFELCTIONS, RECOLLECTIONS & EXPRESSIONS, **(2018).**

ONE, TWO, THREE... ETERNITY: *A Poetic Odyssey,* **2018).**

INDIA: *Journey of Enlightenment (2019).*

SPINNING MIND, SPINNING TIME: *C'est la vie (2019). Book 1.*

MEDITATION ON HOLY TRINITY *(2019), Book 2.*

ENLIGHTENMENT: *Fiat lux* **(2019), Book 3.**

BEING IN THE CONTEXTUAL ORBIT: *Rhythm, Melody & Meaning* **(2019).**

QUINTESSENCE: *Thought & Action* (2019).

THE WILL TO ASCENT: *Power of Boldness & Genius* (2019).

RIDE ON A SPINNING WHEEL: *Existence Introspected* (2020a).

A FLASH OF LIGHT: *Splendors, Perplexities & Riddles* (2020b).

ON A ZIG ZAG TRAIL: *The Flow of Life* (2020c).

UNBOUNDED: *An Inner Sense of Destiny* (2020d).

JAGDISH J. BHATT, PhD

**Brings 45 years of academic experience including
the post-doctorate scientist at Stanford University, CA.
He has authored numerous publications including 28
books which cover the scientific and literary fields.**